J
5/12/07

PHILIP'S
CHILDREN'S PICTURE
ATLAS

Published in Great Britain in 2006
by Philip's,
a division of Octopus Publishing Group Limited,
2–4 Heron Quays, London E14 4JP

ISBN-13   978–0–540–08960–4
ISBN-10   0–540–08960–5

A CIP catalogue record for this book is available from the British Library.

Text: Alison Cooper and Anne McRae
Illustrations: Daniela De Luca
Additional Illustrations: Paola Holguín
Picture Research: Antonella Meucci

Design: Marco Nardi
Layout and cutouts: Adriano Nardi and Ornella Fassio
Editing: Anne McRae and Cath Senker

Printed and bound in Italy

Details of other Philip's titles and services can be found on our website at:
www.philips-maps.co.uk

Contents

Planet Earth

The Earth is a planet in the Solar System, orbiting around the Sun. Millions of years ago, the Solar System was a gigantic cloud of hot gases and particles. Gradually clouds of material joined together to form the Sun and the planets. The way the Earth moves in relation to the Sun affects the seasons and the climate. The way it spins on its axis creates day and night.

North and south

An imaginary horizontal line around the centre of the Earth, called the Equator, divides the planet into the Northern Hemisphere and the Southern Hemisphere. The most northerly point of the Northern Hemisphere is called the North Pole. The South Pole is the most southerly point of the Southern Hemisphere.

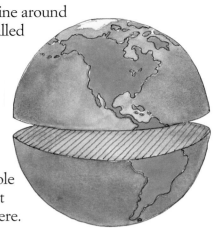

NORTH AND SOUTH

The Solar System

The Solar System is a group of nine planets which orbit the Sun. It takes just over 365 days for the Earth to orbit the Sun. The Moon is a satellite of the Earth. It orbits the Earth every 29.5 days. Some planets have more than one moon – Jupiter has at least 63.

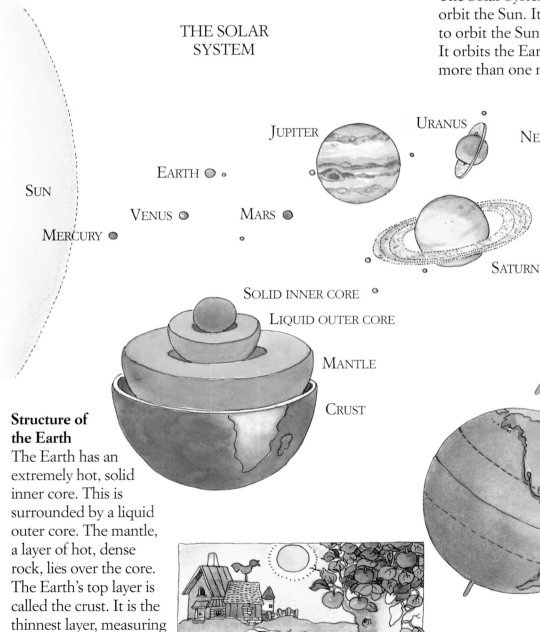

THE SOLAR SYSTEM

SUN

MERCURY

VENUS

EARTH

MARS

JUPITER

URANUS

NEPTUNE

PLUTO

SATURN

SOLID INNER CORE

LIQUID OUTER CORE

MANTLE

CRUST

Structure of the Earth

The Earth has an extremely hot, solid inner core. This is surrounded by a liquid outer core. The mantle, a layer of hot, dense rock, lies over the core. The Earth's top layer is called the crust. It is the thinnest layer, measuring about 60–70 km thick under the mountain ranges, but just 6 km thick under parts of the ocean floor.

Summer

SUMMER IN THE NORTH

WINTER IN THE SOUTH

Summer in the Northern Hemisphere

Now the Northern Hemisphere is tilted towards the Sun. It is summer in the North. It is winter in the South.

Day and night
The Earth turns all the way round on its axis every
24 hours. It is daytime in the half that is facing the Sun.
It is night-time in the half that is turned away from the Sun.

CLIMATIC ZONES

Hot and cold
It is always warmer at the Equator than it is at the North and South Poles. This is because the Earth is round. In the tropical areas near the Equator the Sun's rays hit the Earth almost vertically, making it very hot. Moving away from the Equator, the Sun's rays hit the Earth at an angle and temperatures are lower.

SPRING IN THE NORTH

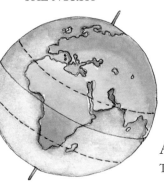

Spring

Winter

AUTUMN IN THE SOUTH

The Seasons
The Earth is tilted on its axis at an angle of about 23.5 degrees. As the Earth moves around the Sun, one hemisphere is tilted towards the Sun and the other is tilted away.

WINTER IN THE NORTH

SUMMER IN THE SOUTH

SUN

Winter in the Northern Hemisphere
The Northern Hemisphere is tilted away from the Sun, so it is winter there. It is summer in the Southern Hemisphere.

AUTUMN IN THE NORTH

Autumn

SPRING IN THE SOUTH

The World

The world is divided into seven continents which are further broken up into more than 190 countries.

GREENLAND (DENMARK)

ALASKA (USA)

ICELAND

DE

NETHER

UNITED KINGDOM

BEL

IRELAND

CANADA

LUXEMBOURG

FR.

SWITZERLAND
LIECHTENSTEIN

AN

PACIFIC OCEAN

UNITED STATES OF AMERICA

ATLANTIC OCEAN

SPAIN

PORTUGAL

MOROCCO

AL

MEXICO

WESTERN SAHARA

CAPE VERDE

MAURITANIA

MAL

HAWAIIAN ISLANDS

BAHAMAS

DOMINICAN REPUBLIC

PUERTO RICO (USA)

CUBA

HAITI

JAMAICA

BELIZE

HONDURAS

GUATEMALA

EL SALVADOR

NICARAGUA

ANTIGUA & BARBUDA
ST KITTS & NEVIS
ST LUCIA

DOMINICA
GRENADA

ST VINCENT & THE GRENADINES

BARBADOS

TRINIDAD & TOBAGO

SENEGAL

GAMBIA
GUINEA-
BISSAU

GUINEA

SIERRA LEONE

BURKINA
FASO

IVORY COAST

LIBERIA

COSTA RICA

PANAMA

VENEZUELA

GUYANA

FRENCH GUIANA

COLOMBIA

ECUADOR

SURINAME

TOGO

SÃO TOMÉ
& PRÍNCIPE

EQUATORI
GUINEA

GABON

CON

North America

North America's highest mountain is Mount McKinley in Alaska (6,194 m). At 86 metres below sea-level, Death Valley in California is the continent's lowest point. Lake Superior, the largest and deepest of the Great Lakes, is the second-largest lake in the world. The Niagara Falls is one of the world's biggest waterfalls.

BRAZIL

PERU

BOLIVIA

PARAGUAY

CHILE

URUGUAY

ARGENTINA

South America

The highest mountain in South America is Aconcagua in Argentina (6,962 m). Venezuela has the world's highest waterfall, the Angel Falls, with a drop of 979 metres. The Amazon River in Brazil is the second-longest river in the world.

Antarctica

Surrounding the South Pole and bordered by the southern regions of the Atlantic, Pacific and Indian Oceans, Antarctica is a snowy desert and cold all year round. Greenland in the Arctic Ocean is the world's largest island.

Europe
Mont Blanc in the Alps, on the border between France and Italy, is the highest mountain in Europe (4,807 m). The River Volga in Russia is Europe's longest river, and the Caspian Sea is the world's largest lake. Russia is the biggest country in the world.

Asia
The Himalayas, which run across the border between India, China and Nepal, are the world's highest mountains. The tallest peak of all is Mount Everest (8,850 m). With over 1,250 million people, China has more inhabitants than any other country in the world. Japan's highest mountain is Mount Fuji (3,776 m).

Africa
The River Nile in Egypt and Sudan is the longest river in the world. Africa also has the world's biggest desert, the Sahara, which covers around 9 million square kilometres. Air temperatures here have reached 58°C, the highest ever recorded. Africa's highest mountain is Mount Kilimanjaro in Tanzania (5,895 m).

Australasia is made up of Australia, New Zealand and the islands in the southern Pacific Ocean. Australia is the smallest of the continents. It is also the driest, apart from Antarctica, and the flattest. The highest mountain in Australasia is Aoraki Mount Cook, on New Zealand's South Island (3,753 m).

9

What is a Map?

A map is a way of presenting information about a place. Many different kinds of information can be shown on a map, so it is important to use the right type of map when you are trying to find out something. If you want to know where Nigeria is, you need to look at a map of the world in an atlas. But an atlas would be no use to you if you wanted to go out for a walk. For this you would need a large-scale map that shows small features such as footpaths and houses.

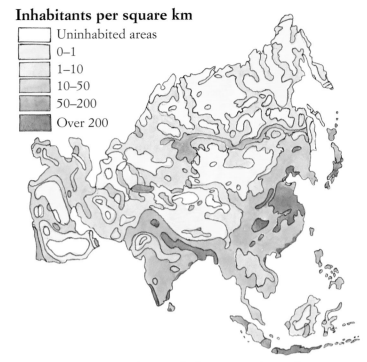

A **population map** shows how many people live in an area. These maps usually have a coloured key showing the density of population in each area.

Physical maps show rivers, lakes, mountains, deserts, areas of flat land and other physical features of the landscape. They do not usually show the borders of the countries or settlements and transport routes. A topographic map shows both physical and man-made features.

Political maps usually show each country or region in a different colour. You can use these maps to find out what part of the world a country is in and how big or small it is. Political maps sometimes show where towns and cities are too.

Economic maps show how the land is used and the main types of work that are carried out in a country or region. These maps often have picture symbols and a key to explain them.

Fishing
Sheep farming
Cattle raising
Cereal growing
Grapes
Mining
Diamonds
Farming and forestry
Arid farmland
Desert

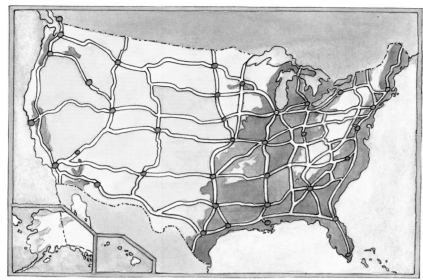

If you are planning a car journey, you need a **road map**. Road maps show the routes that link cities and towns. They usually show different types of road in different colours, so that you can quickly tell whether a road is a country lane or a motorway.

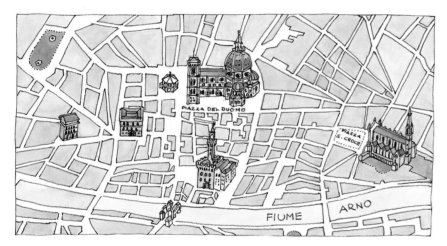

Bus or underground maps show the routes and how they connect with one another. They do not show the twists and turns of the roads and tunnels – the networks are simplified so it is easy to see how to get from one place to another.

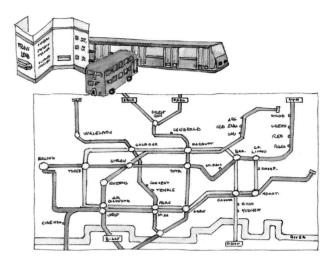

Tourist maps are large-scale maps of a region or a city. They show the road networks and usually include picture symbols showing places to visit. They can help you find places such as museums, art galleries, churches, parks, gardens, restaurants and hotels.

Looking at **old maps** is a good way to find out how places have changed over the centuries. New towns and roads are built and old settlements disappear. Even the shape of the coastline changes over time. Maps are much more accurate than they used to be.

Stars are divided into groups called constellations. **Star maps** show the constellations and their positions in the sky.

Ursa Major, the Great Bear, is the third-largest constellation in the sky.

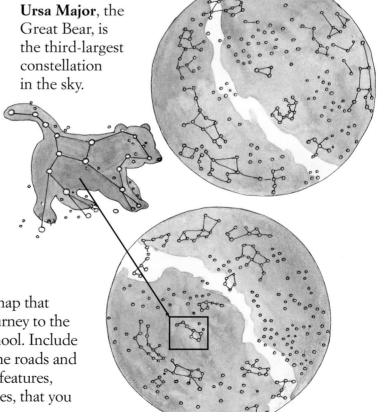

Try making a map that shows your journey to the shops or to school. Include the names of the roads and any important features, such as churches, that you pass on the way.

Savannas are areas of tropical grassland, with a few trees here and there. The climate is hot and quite dry. Animals that live on the savanna include elephants, giraffes, zebras and lions.

Tropical forests are found in a broad band around the Equator. Here the climate is hot and very wet. There is a rich variety of plant and animal life – monkeys, tree frogs, snakes, and birds such as toucans and parrots.

Vast **coniferous forests** stretch across the northern part of the world, in Europe, Asia and North America. Conifers thrive in cold, dry conditions. The snow slides off their sloping branches instead of breaking them with its weight. Wolves, elks and beavers are some of the animals that live in these forests.

In areas that have mild, damp climates there are **deciduous woodlands**. Trees such as oaks, beeches and maples produce new leaves in spring and lose them each autumn. Creatures that live in woodlands include foxes, deer, stoats, squirrels, owls and woodpeckers.

Human environments are shaped by the people who live there. They cut down woodland, drain marshes and irrigate deserts, so that they can farm the land and build settlements. They introduce new species of animals.

Deserts are very dry areas. Camels, fennec foxes and scorpions are desert animals. Most deserts are not sandy, and they are not always hot. The Gobi Desert in China is very hot in summer, but in winter it is bitterly cold.

High in the **mountains** the air is cold, even in areas where it is hot in the lowlands. The lower slopes are often covered in forests, but near the peaks there is bare rock or snow. Mountain animals include wild sheep and goats. Birds of prey, such as eagles, soar overhead.

Mediterranean regions have hot, dry summers and mild, wet winters. Plants tend to be low-growing shrubs such as lavender and thyme, and trees such as olives and cork oaks. They can survive with very little water in the summer months. Few large mammals live in these regions, but there are many species of insects and birds.

Many **rivers** are rich in fish in their lowland sections, just before they reach the sea. Perch, roach and bream are common species of freshwater fish. **Lakes** are home to fish, and birds such as kingfishers, herons, ducks and grebes.

Over 70 per cent of the Earth's surface is covered in water. Brightly-coloured tropical fish dart among the coral reefs in warm **ocean** waters. The icy Southern Ocean around Antarctica is home to the blue whale, the world's largest mammal. In the very deepest parts of the oceans there are strange creatures that live in total darkness. The ocean depths are the last unexplored areas of our planet.

The world has many different environments, with different climates, landscapes, plants and animals. The map shows where the main environments are located.

World Environments

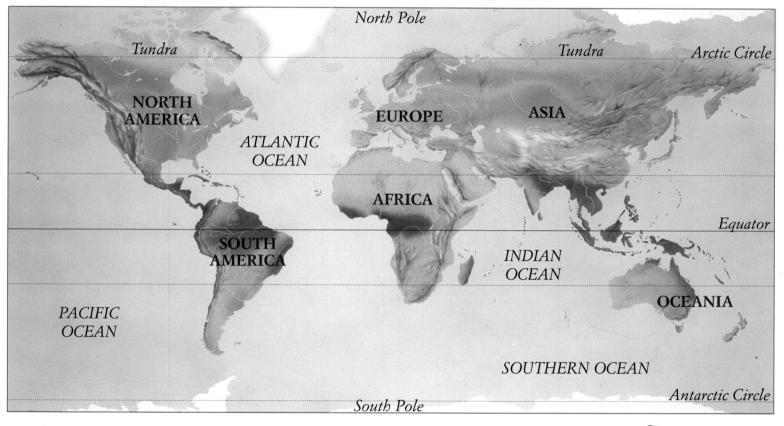

In **polar regions** temperatures are mostly below freezing. Polar animals have thick fur or blubber to keep warm. Along the northern coasts of North America, Europe and Asia lies the **tundra**. Here the snow melts briefly in summer, and lichens, mosses and small shrubs bloom. Reindeer and arctic foxes are tundra animals.

Islands often have unique species of plants and animals. This is because they have been separated from mainland species and have developed in a different way. Plant seeds and insects are carried to islands on air currents or in the water. Animals are sometimes carried to islands by passing ships.

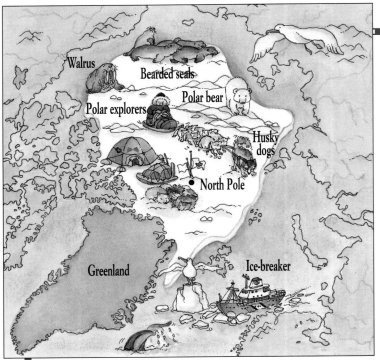

Walrus
Bearded seals
Polar explorers
Polar bear
Husky dogs
North Pole
Greenland
Ice-breaker

◆ CANADA, ALASKA AND THE ARCTIC

Canada is an independent country. Alaska is a state of the United States and Greenland belongs to Denmark, although it is self-governing. Find the capital cities of Canada and Greenland and the largest city in Alaska on the map.

1 Ottawa   **2** Nuuk (Godthab)   **3** Juneau

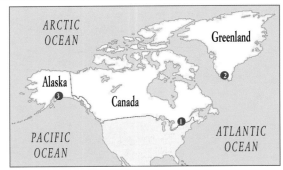

ARCTIC OCEAN
Greenland
Alaska
Canada
PACIFIC OCEAN
ATLANTIC OCEAN

The Arctic
No one lives on the drifting Arctic ice, although some people go there to hunt and explore. The North Pole is on the frozen ice.

The Arctic is an ocean. Part of it is covered with drifting ice, some of which never melts. The surrounding land is covered with ice and snow all year round. Further south, flowers bloom on the tundra during the short summer. Beyond the tundra there are great forests and plains. Canada's Great Slave Lake and Great Bear Lake are among the biggest lakes in the world. The St Lawrence River is an important transport route in the east.

USA
ATLANTIC OCEAN
PACIFIC OCEAN
South America

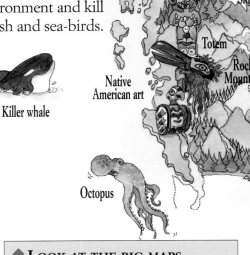

Auk
Walrus
Caribou
Yukon River
Oi
Gold mining
Mackenzie River
Bering Strait
Polar willow
Pipeline
Humpback whale
Kodiak bears
Pike
Aleutian Islands
Dalls sheep
Wolf
Grizzly bear
Salmon
Rocky Mountain goat
Seaplane
Swan
Pipelines and pollution

Pipelines and pollution
The Trans-Alaska pipeline snakes across the tundra, carrying oil from the drilling sites to coastal ports. Oil is important to the economy, but there are dangers. Oil spills often cause serious damage to the environment and kill thousands of fish and sea-birds.

Killer whale
Native American art
Skiing
Totem
Rocky Mountains
Octopus

Canada, Alaska and the Arctic

Canada is the second-biggest country in the world, but it is one of the least crowded. Very few people live in the icy Arctic regions of the north. Further south, most people live in towns and cities. Farming, forestry, and fishing are important types of work. The main language is English but there are also many French speakers. In the Arctic, the biggest group of people are the Inuit. In the past they survived by hunting and trapping animals for their fur. Now, many work in the mining and oil-drilling industries.

◆ **LOOK AT THE BIG MAPS.**
Can you find…
• four different kinds of whale?
• the North Pole?
• two large rivers?
• three types of sport?
• the Rocky Mountains?
• Bering Strait?

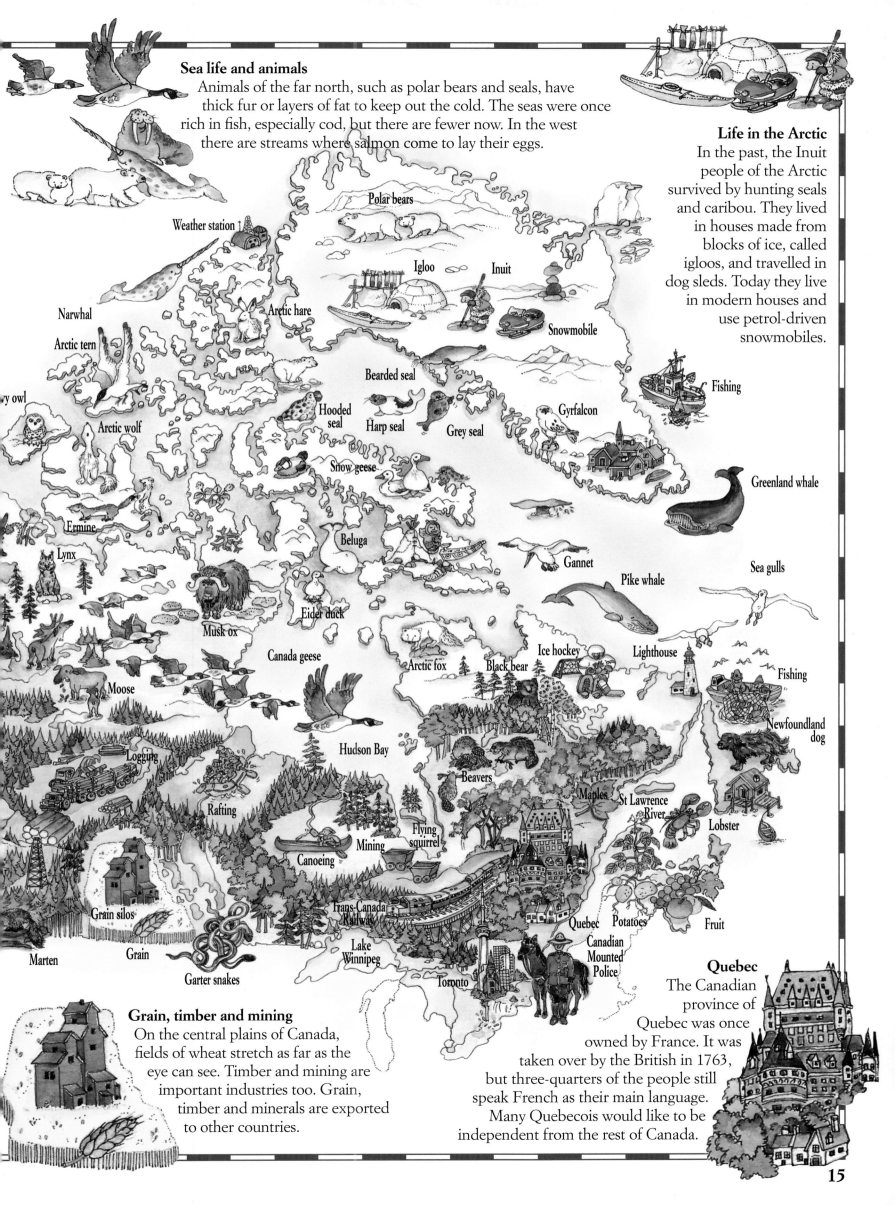

Sea life and animals

Animals of the far north, such as polar bears and seals, have thick fur or layers of fat to keep out the cold. The seas were once rich in fish, especially cod, but there are fewer now. In the west there are streams where salmon come to lay their eggs.

Life in the Arctic

In the past, the Inuit people of the Arctic survived by hunting seals and caribou. They lived in houses made from blocks of ice, called igloos, and travelled in dog sleds. Today they live in modern houses and use petrol-driven snowmobiles.

Grain, timber and mining

On the central plains of Canada, fields of wheat stretch as far as the eye can see. Timber and mining are important industries too. Grain, timber and minerals are exported to other countries.

Quebec

The Canadian province of Quebec was once owned by France. It was taken over by the British in 1763, but three-quarters of the people still speak French as their main language. Many Quebecois would like to be independent from the rest of Canada.

Map labels:
Polar bears, Weather station, Igloo, Inuit, Snowmobile, Narwhal, Arctic hare, Arctic tern, Fishing, owl, Arctic wolf, Bearded seal, Gyrfalcon, Hooded seal, Harp seal, Grey seal, Snow geese, Greenland whale, Ermine, Beluga, Gannet, Sea gulls, Lynx, Pike whale, Eider duck, Musk ox, Canada geese, Arctic fox, Black bear, Ice hockey, Lighthouse, Fishing, Moose, Newfoundland dog, Logging, Hudson Bay, Beavers, Maples, St Lawrence River, Rafting, Flying squirrel, Lobster, Canoeing, Mining, Quebec, Potatoes, Fruit, Grain silos, Trans-Canada Railway, Lake Winnipeg, Canadian Mounted Police, Marten, Grain, Garter snakes, Toronto

The landscape and climate of the USA are very varied. To the west are the snowy peaks of the Rocky Mountains. On the plains of the Mid-West, summers are warm but winters are cold and snowy. In the south-west, there are hot, dry deserts. The islands of Hawaii are also part of the USA.

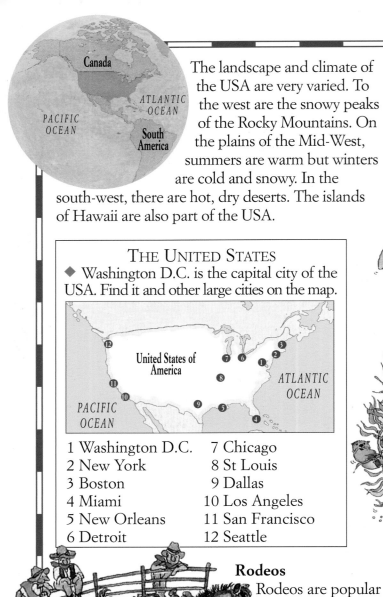

THE UNITED STATES

◆ Washington D.C. is the capital city of the USA. Find it and other large cities on the map.

United States of America

ATLANTIC OCEAN

PACIFIC OCEAN

1 Washington D.C.   7 Chicago
2 New York   8 St Louis
3 Boston   9 Dallas
4 Miami   10 Los Angeles
5 New Orleans   11 San Francisco
6 Detroit   12 Seattle

Rodeos

Rodeos are popular events in the West. Cowboys show off their skills at calf-roping, bull-riding, and riding untrained horses – the famous bucking broncos!

The United States

The United States of America is the richest and most powerful country in the world. It is made up of 50 states. Each state has its own local government and makes its own laws. English is the main language. Most people live in towns or cities, and work in shops, offices, factories and service industries. The USA has some very big cities, such as New York and Los Angeles, but there are large areas of the country where very few people live.

Surfing

Tourism

THE ISLANDS OF HAWAII

Volcanoes

To the Moon!

In 1969 Apollo 11 blasted off from Cape Canaveral, taking men to the Moon for the first time. Space and aircraft technology, computers and military equipment are all important industries in the USA.

Apples
Rocky Mountain goat
Bison
Aeroplane
Grey whale
Quail
Porcupine
Branding iron
Chipmunk
Wapiti
Condor
Hare
Giant redwood
Potatoes
Big horn sheep
Grizzly bears
San Francisco
Salt Lake
Mustang
Lynx
Speedway
Otters
Computer
Las Vegas
Garibaldi fish
Fruit
Grand Canyon
Puma
Plums
Winter sports
Hollywood
Movies
Elf owl
Road runner
Navajo weaving
Elephant seals
Joshua tree
Cactus
Copper
Colorado River
Rattlesnake
Chuckwalla
Horned lizard
Rio Grande River

The American Dream
During the last 500 years, more than 60 million people from all over the world have come to live in the United States. They come in search of wealth and freedom.

The Pilgrim Fathers
The Pilgrim Fathers were among the first settlers from Europe. They set sail from England in the *Mayflower* in 1620. They hoped that in America they would be free to worship God in the way they wanted. They set up the colony of Plymouth, Massachusetts.

Wheat
Bald eagle
Missouri River
Loon
Mount Rushmore
Beetroot
American black bear
Virginia deer
Dairy cow
Barley
Farm
Gold
Prairie dogs
Skunks
Sunflowers
Corn
Basketball
Chicago
St Louis
Farmstead
Cereals
Turkey
Racoon
American football
Coyote
Gas
Oil
Pike
Paddle boat
Oil
Rodeo
Cotton
Oil
Alligator turtle
Plantation house
Mississippi River
New Orleans Jazz
Water melon
Cattle
Manatees
Spoonbill
Crane
Lake Superior
Trout
Salmon
Lake Huron
Lake Michigan
Cherries
Car making
Farm
Pigs
Bourbon
Opossum
Horses
Soya
Blueberries
Cotton
Snake
Everglades
Alligator
Niagara Falls
Lake Erie
Tomatoes
Mines
Tobacco
Peanuts
Snakebird
Fir trees
Maple tree and syrup
Cranberries
Halloween pumpkin
Oak tree
Beaver
Statue of Liberty
New York
Washington D.C.
Scissorbill
Whale
Pelican
Lighthouse
Heron
Cape Canaveral
Tourism
Marlin

Sports
Basketball and baseball developed in the USA. They are now enjoyed by people in many countries. American football is not played much outside the USA. Every year millions of Americans watch the championship finals, the Super Bowl, on television.

◆ **LOOK AT THE BIG MAP.**
Can you find…
• the Statue of Liberty?
• five different kinds of wild animal?
• two large rivers and Niagara Falls?
• five different kinds of fruit?

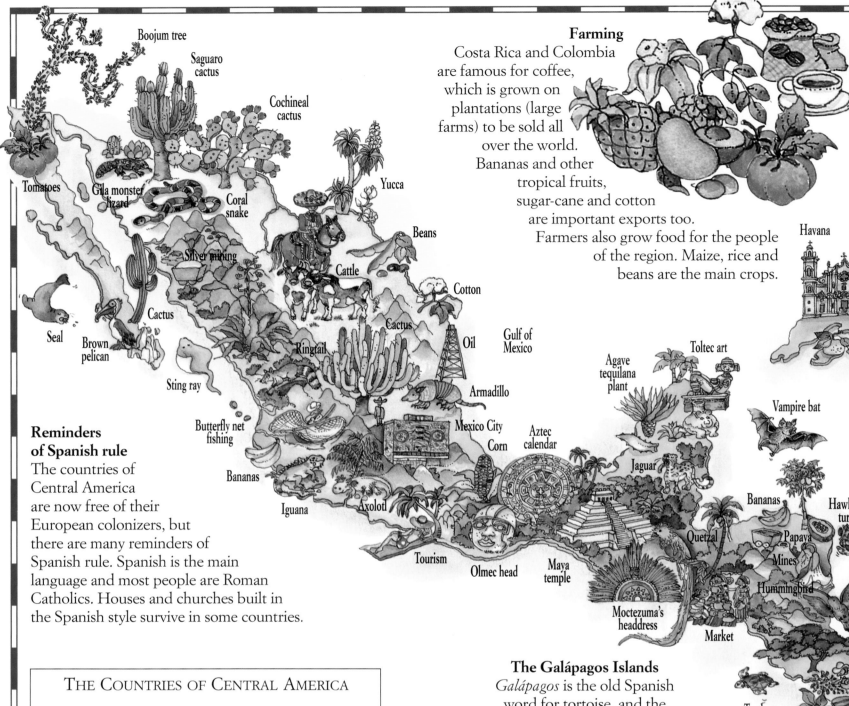

Farming
Costa Rica and Colombia are famous for coffee, which is grown on plantations (large farms) to be sold all over the world. Bananas and other tropical fruits, sugar-cane and cotton are important exports too.
Farmers also grow food for the people of the region. Maize, rice and beans are the main crops.

Boojum tree

Saguaro cactus

Cochineal cactus

Yucca

Tomatoes

Gila monster lizard

Coral snake

Beans

Silver mining

Cattle

Cotton

Cactus

Seal

Brown pelican

Ringtail

Cactus

Oil

Gulf of Mexico

Havana

Sting ray

Armadillo

Butterfly net fishing

Mexico City

Aztec calendar

Corn

Agave tequilana plant

Toltec art

Vampire bat

Bananas

Iguana

Axolotl

Bananas

Hawks turtle

Jaguar

Quetzal

Papaya

Mines

Reminders of Spanish rule
The countries of Central America are now free of their European colonizers, but there are many reminders of Spanish rule. Spanish is the main language and most people are Roman Catholics. Houses and churches built in the Spanish style survive in some countries.

Tourism

Olmec head

Maya temple

Moctezuma's headdress

Hummingbird

Market

The Galápagos Islands
Galápagos is the old Spanish word for tortoise, and the giant tortoises are the islands' most famous inhabitants.

Turtle

Coffee

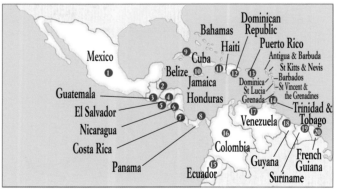

THE COUNTRIES OF CENTRAL AMERICA

◆ Match the names with the numbers on the map to find the capital cities of the larger countries.

Mexico

Bahamas

Dominican Republic

Haiti

Puerto Rico

Cuba

Antigua & Barbuda

St Kitts & Nevis

Belize

Jamaica

Dominica

St Lucia

Barbados

St Vincent & the Grenadines

Guatemala

Honduras

Grenada

El Salvador

Trinidad & Tobago

Nicaragua

Venezuela

Costa Rica

Colombia

Guyana

French Guiana

Panama

Ecuador

Suriname

1 Mexico City	8 Panama City	14 Port-of-Spain
2 Belmopan	9 Havana	15 Quito
3 Guatemala City	10 Kingston	16 Bogotá
4 Tegucigalpa	11 Port-au-Prince	17 Caracas
5 San Salvador	12 Santo	18 Georgetown
6 Managua	Domingo	19 Paramaribo
7 San José	13 San Juan	20 Cayenne

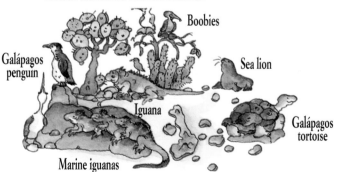

Galápagos penguin

Boobies

Sea lion

Iguana

Marine iguanas

Galápagos tortoise

Maya and Aztecs
The Maya lived in what are now Guatemala, Honduras and Belize. They built cities with huge stone pyramids and temples. Later, the Aztecs controlled a large empire from the great city of Tenochtitlan. Their empire was destroyed by the Spanish in 1521.

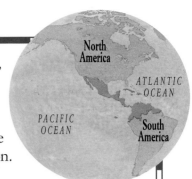

◆ **LOOK AT THE BIG MAP.**
Can you find…
- three examples of Maya or Aztec art?
- ten different wild animals?
- ten different types of fruit?
- the Galápagos Islands?
- the Panama Canal?

Most of Central America is hilly or mountainous, although there are humid swamps along the eastern coasts. There are tropical rainforests in Central America and northern South America. The region lies on a fault in the Earth's crust, so there are many volcanoes here and earthquakes can cause terrible destruction.

Mexico and Central America

The countries of Central America form a 'bridge' linking North and South America. Most people in the region have Native American and European ancestors, because much of the area was ruled by Spain in colonial times. Many people work as farmers, or in workshops producing clothing, shoes and furniture. In Mexico there are more people who work in factories.

Brown pelican
Tropical fruit
Tourism
Cuban cigar
Cuban solenodon
Sugar-cane
Rum
Sailfish
Shark
Coral reefs
Sugar-cane
Caracas
Banana
Oil
Salt mines
Scarlet ibis
Piranha fish
Coconuts
Capybara
Orinoco River
Hoatzin
Mangroves
Harpy eagle
Panama Canal
Cacao
Howler monkey
Emerald
Cattle farming
Bird spider
King vulture
Cayman
Butterfly
Prawns
Gold
Orchid
Spectacled bear
Angel Falls
Ocelot
Pre-Colombian statue
Bogota
Spider monkey
Frogs
ask
Toucans
Sloth
Coati
Coffee
Scarlet macaw
Jaguar
Woolly monkey
Boa
Two-toed anteater
Volcanoes
Poison-arrow frog
Tapir
Panama hat

Jungle animals
Monkeys, toucans and parakeets chatter in the trees of the Colombian jungle. Boa constrictors slither along the branches. Jaguars, the American big cats, stalk their prey. Capybaras – the world's largest rodents – and anteaters snuffle around the jungle floor. Flesh-eating piranhas and crocodiles lurk in the rivers.

South America and Antarctica

Almost half the population of South America lives in Brazil. The main language is Portuguese, because Brazil was once ruled by Portugal. Other countries were ruled by Spain, so Spanish is the main language in the rest of the region. In big cities, such as Rio de Janeiro and Buenos Aires, many people work in factories. Outside the cities farming is the main occupation. Beyond the southern tip of South America lies the frozen continent of Antarctica.

The Andes Mountains run down the western side of South America. To the east, the great Amazon River flows through lush tropical rainforests. In Argentina there are large areas of open grassland, called the Pampas, which are good for farming and raising cattle. The northern part of the continent is warm and wet, but it is cold in the high Andes and in southern Argentina and Chile.

Antarctica

Antarctica is a huge, frozen continent. Very few creatures can survive the extreme cold. Seals and penguins live around the coasts and the oceans are rich in fish. The enormous blue whale, the largest mammal in the world, lives in these icy waters. No one lives permanently in Antarctica, although some scientists stay for a few months to carry out research.

◆ **LOOK AT THE BIG MAPS.**
Can you find…
• the Amazon River?
• six colourful birds?
• four different whales?
• the city of Rio de Janeiro?
• the South Pole?
• four different seals that live in Antarctica?

Cotton

Llamas
Together with alpaca, vicuña, and guanaco, llamas are members of the camel family. They are important to the people of the Andes. They carry loads, provide meat for food, and wool to make clothes, rugs and ropes.

Rainforests
The Amazon rainforest covers 40 per cent of Brazil's total area. Millions of plant and animal species live in the forest. Although the rainforest is important for world climate, large areas are cut down each year to clear land for farming and to provide timber.

Sheathbill
Petrel
Supply ship
Blue whale
Krill
Crabeater seal
Sea lion
Albatross
Emperor penguins
Elephant seal
Research station
Iceberg
South Pole
Wendell seal
Arctic tern
Leopard seal
Camp
Cod
Adélie penguins

THE COUNTRIES OF SOUTH AMERICA

◆ Find the capital cities of each country.

Colombia, Ecuador, Venezuela, Guyana, French Guiana and Suriname are also part of South America. They are on pages 18–19.

1 Brasilia
2 Asunción
3 Lima
4 Santiago
5 Buenos Aires
6 La Paz
7 Montevideo

ATLANTIC OCEAN
Peru
Brazil
Bolivia
Paraguay
Chile
Uruguay
Argentina
SOUTHERN OCEAN

North America
ATLANTIC OCEAN
PACIFIC OCEAN

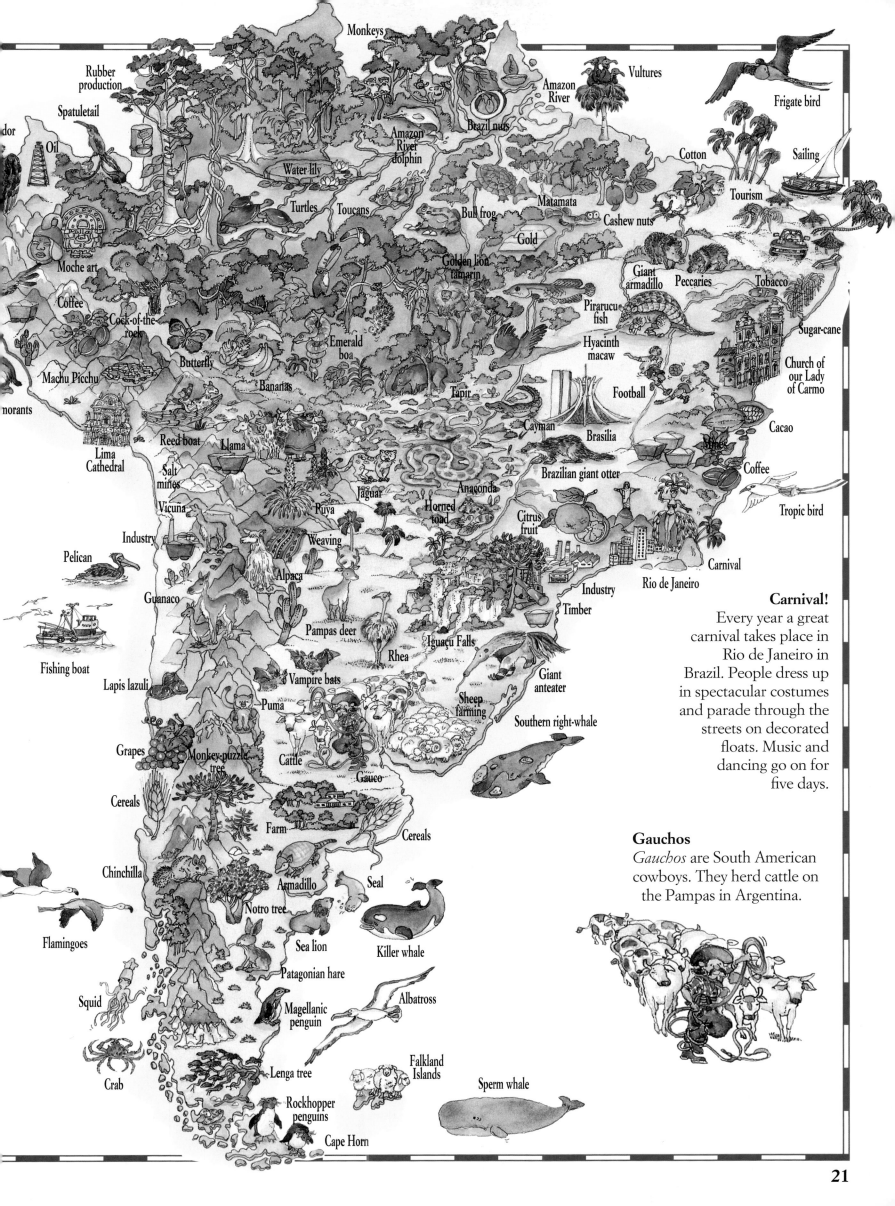

Monkeys

Rubber
production

Spatuletail

...dor

Oil

Vultures

Amazon
River

Frigate bird

Brazil nuts

Cotton

Sailing

Tourism

Amazon
River
dolphin

Water lily

Moche art

Turtles

Toucans

Matamata

Cashew nuts

Gold

Coffee

Cock-of-the-
rock

Butterfly

Golden lion
tamarin

Giant
armadillo

Peccaries

Tobacco

Pirarucu
fish

Sugar-cane

Machu Picchu

Emerald
boa

Hyacinth
macaw

Church of
our Lady
of Carmo

...norants

Bananas

Tapir

Football

Cacao

Lima
Cathedral

Reed boat

Llama

Cayman

Brasilia

Mines

Coffee

Salt
mines

Jaguar

Anaconda

Brazilian giant otter

Tropic bird

Vicuña

Puya

Horned
toad

Citrus
fruit

Industry

Weaving

Carnival

Pelican

Alpaca

Rio de Janeiro

Guanaco

Industry

Timber

Pampas deer

Iguaçu Falls

Fishing boat

Rhea

Giant
anteater

Lapis lazuli

Vampire bats

Sheep
farming

Southern right-whale

Puma

Grapes

Monkey-puzzle
tree

Cattle

Gaucho

Cereals

Farm

Cereals

Chinchilla

Armadillo

Seal

Notro tree

Flamingoes

Sea lion

Killer whale

Patagonian hare

Squid

Albatross

Crab

Magellanic
penguin

Lenga tree

Falkland
Islands

Sperm whale

Rockhopper
penguins

Cape Horn

Carnival!
Every year a great
carnival takes place in
Rio de Janeiro in
Brazil. People dress up
in spectacular costumes
and parade through the
streets on decorated
floats. Music and
dancing go on for
five days.

Gauchos
Gauchos are South American
cowboys. They herd cattle on
the Pampas in Argentina.

21

Northern Europe

Northern Europe is composed of the four Nordic countries of Finland, Norway, Sweden and Denmark, as well as the United Kingdom, Ireland and Iceland. There is a lot of industry, and most people work in factories, offices, shops and service industries. Fishing and farming are also important activities. English is the main language in the United Kingdom and Ireland. The Nordic countries each have their own language.

Tourism
Tourism is important in Scotland. People come to see the beautiful scenery and to enjoy Scottish traditions, such as bagpipe music and tartan kilts.

A great past
There are many old castles, churches and stately homes in the United Kingdom and Ireland.

The countries of **northern Europe** have cool climates with high rainfall. They have long, cold winters, particularly in the north. In Iceland and the north of the Nordic countries it stays dark all day during the winter months. In summer, it is light even at night.

Puffin
Volcano
Waterfall
Walrus
Seals
Killer whale

ARCTIC OCEAN
ATLANTIC OCEAN
Europe
Africa

Faroe Islands
Sheep
Shetland Islands

Tweed
Fisherman
Duck
Orkney Islands
Hebrides Islands
Bagpipes
Cormorant
Whisky
Kilts
Loch Ness monster
Sea gulls
Fisherman
Celtic cross
Castle
Hake
Sheep
Collie
Lobster
Irish setter
Horse
Shipbuilding yards
Ceramics
Heather
Isle of Man
Factory
Beer
Cottage
Guinness
Soccer
Woods
Peat
Potatoes
Barley
Mines
Horse riding
Cow
Student
Fox
Herrings
Welsh costume
Manor house
Tower Bridge
Daffodils
Stonehenge
River Thames
Salisbury Cathedral
Badger
Fish
Dog fish
Channel Islands

22

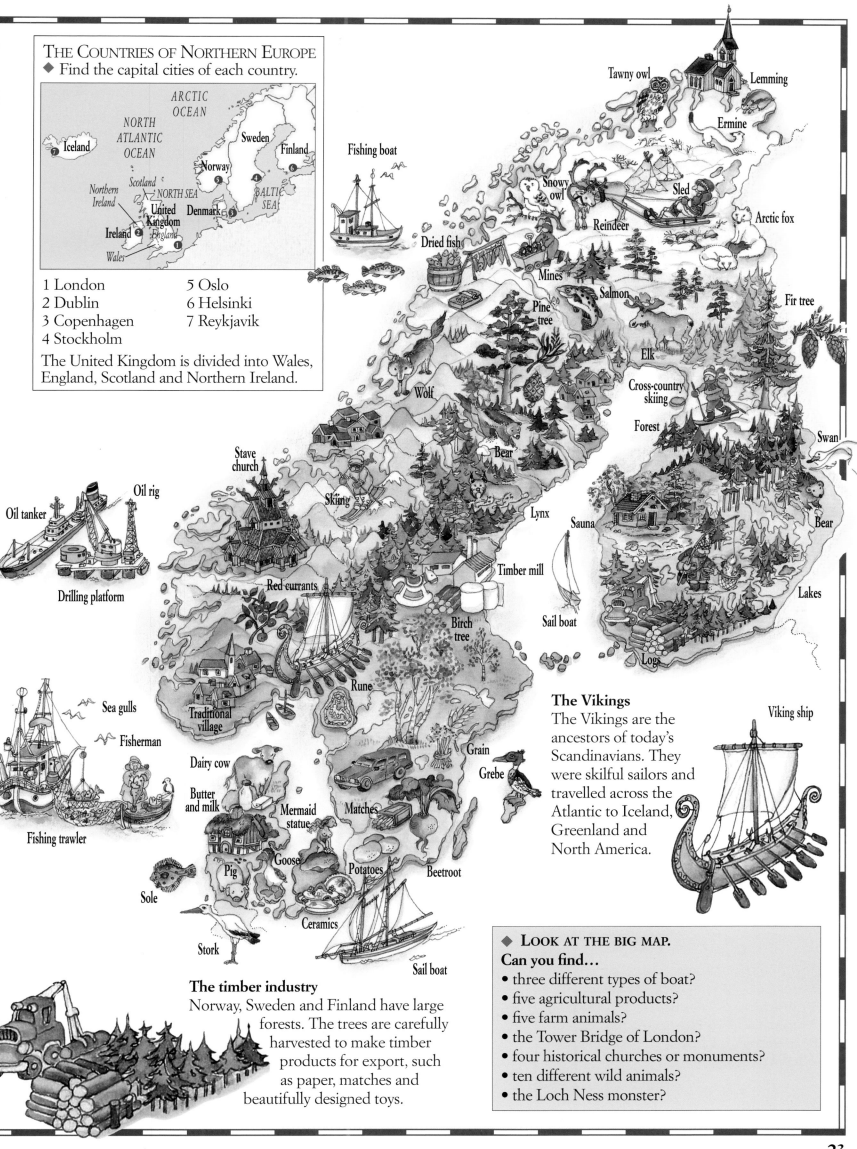

THE COUNTRIES OF NORTHERN EUROPE
◆ Find the capital cities of each country.

ARCTIC OCEAN
NORTH ATLANTIC OCEAN
Iceland 7
Sweden
Norway
Finland 6
Scotland
NORTH SEA
5
4
Northern Ireland
United Kingdom
Denmark 3
BALTIC SEA
England 1
Ireland 2
Wales

1 London
2 Dublin
3 Copenhagen
4 Stockholm
5 Oslo
6 Helsinki
7 Reykjavik

The United Kingdom is divided into Wales, England, Scotland and Northern Ireland.

Fishing boat
Tawny owl
Lemming
Ermine
Snowy owl
Sled
Reindeer
Arctic fox
Dried fish
Mines
Salmon
Pine tree
Fir tree
Elk
Cross-country skiing
Forest
Wolf
Swan
Bear
Lynx
Sauna
Bear
Oil rig
Oil tanker
Drilling platform
Timber mill
Lakes
Skiing
Stave church
Red currants
Birch tree
Logs
Sail boat
Rune

The Vikings
The Vikings are the ancestors of today's Scandinavians. They were skilful sailors and travelled across the Atlantic to Iceland, Greenland and North America.

Viking ship

Sea gulls
Fisherman
Grain
Grebe
Dairy cow
Butter and milk
Matches
Mermaid statue
Fishing trawler
Goose
Potatoes
Beetroot
Pig
Sole
Ceramics
Stork
Sail boat

The timber industry
Norway, Sweden and Finland have large forests. The trees are carefully harvested to make timber products for export, such as paper, matches and beautifully designed toys.

◆ **LOOK AT THE BIG MAP.**
Can you find…
• three different types of boat?
• five agricultural products?
• five farm animals?
• the Tower Bridge of London?
• four historical churches or monuments?
• ten different wild animals?
• the Loch Ness monster?

23

Central Europe

Most people in central Europe live in towns and cities and work in offices and factories. The factories produce a wide range of goods, from cars in Germany to watches and medical instruments in Switzerland. Farming is also important in some areas, especially southern Germany and parts of the Netherlands. German is spoken in several countries but each country has its own language.

◆ **LOOK AT THE BIG MAP.**
Can you find…
• Vienna and the Lipizzaner horse?
• two large ports?
• five wild animals?
• three different types of food?

Beer and wine
Barley and hops are grown in Germany to make beer. A famous beer festival, the *Oktoberfest*, is held each year in Munich to celebrate the harvest. There are also many vineyards where grapes are grown and made into wine.

THE COUNTRIES OF CENTRAL EUROPE
◆ Find the capital cities of each country.

1 Amsterdam	5 Bern	9 Prague
2 Brussels	6 Vienna	10 Bratislava
3 Luxembourg	7 Vaduz	11 Budapest
4 Berlin	8 Warsaw	

The Rhine

The Rhine is the biggest river in central Europe. It flows for 1,392 km from the Swiss Alps to the Netherlands, where it empties into the North Sea. Barges loaded with cargo travel along the Rhine, calling at inland ports, such as Cologne. In Switzerland, the energy of its rushing waters is used to produce hydroelectric power.

Vienna

Vienna is the capital of Austria. It was once the centre of a powerful empire. Beautiful old buildings, such as the Imperial Palace, are reminders of its past. Acrobatic Lipizzaner horses are trained at the Spanish Riding School. The Vienna State Opera is one of the most famous opera houses in the world.

East and West

Poland, the Czech Republic, Slovakia, Hungary and eastern Germany were ruled by Communist governments under the influence of the Soviet Union until the late 1980s. Germany was divided into two separate countries. When Communism collapsed in 1989–90, Germany became one country again. People flocked to the wall that divided Berlin and tore it down.

The landscape of central Europe is varied. The Netherlands is very flat – parts of the country are below sea-level and have to be drained by a system of dykes. Switzerland and Austria, in the south, are mountainous. The mountains here are the Alps. The Carpathian Mountains are further east, in southern Poland and Slovakia. The River Rhine and the River Danube flow across the centre of the region.

Stork

Container loader

Port

Black stork

Cod

Herring

Amber

River Oder

Gdansk

River Vistula

Elk

Farming

European bison

Potatoes

Beet

Lapwings

Carp

Coal mining

Brandenburg Gate

Cuckoo

Red deer

Roe deer

Warsaw

Wooden house

Grey heron

Dormouse

Elm tree

Hare

Barley

Icon

Crows

Wheat

Owl

Industry

Mole

Dresden

Mountaineering

Kraków

Wooden church

Traditional costume

Chamois goat

Otter

Lynx

Prague

Thermal springs

Brown bear

Coal

Industry

Bohemian crystal

Barley

Grapes

Bratislava

Timber

Wild boars

Industry

Vienna

Wine

Lipizzaner horse

Shepherd

Vulture

Spoonbill

Catfish

Budapest

Hungarian horseman

Paprika

Beet

Water vole

Corn

River Danube

Polecat

Southern Europe

Many parts of southern Europe have big cities, and a lot of industry. The people in these areas work in factories, offices and shops. They have modern lifestyles. In some other areas the people live as farmers. They lead traditional lives, just as their parents and grandparents did.

Punch
The famous puppet called Punch first came from Italy. In Italian he is called *Pulcinella*.

The countries of **southern Europe** face across the Mediterranean Sea towards Africa. The region has many mountains. The largest ranges are the Alps in northern Italy, and the Pyrenees between Spain and France. There are many rivers, the largest of which is the Loire, in France. The winters are quite mild and wet, while the summers are hot and dry. There are some large forests in the north. There are many islands in the Mediterranean Sea. The Italian islands of Sicily and Sardinia are the largest.

Europe
Asia
ATLANTIC OCEAN
Africa
INDIAN OCEAN

Oysters
Mont Saint-Michel
Port
Car factory
River Seine
Farm
Hedgehog
Goose
Mines
Notre-Dame
Cow
Champagne
River Loire
Snail
Chateaux
Cheese
Acorn
River Garonne
TGV
Wine
Ceramics
Tunnel
Surfer
Mont Blanc
Owl
Cave paintings
Fox
Apples
Eagle
Santiago de Compostela
Pyrenees
Camargue horse
Vinyards
River Rhône
Partridges
Lavender
Hare
Sardines
River Douro
Deer
Sagrada Familia Church
River Tagus
Oak
Bull fighter
Duck
Escorial Palace
River Ebro
Windmills
Lobster
Tourism
Sheep
Balearic Islands
Seal
Lynx
Heron
Apricots
River Guadiana
River Guadalquivir
Tuna
Alhambra
Flamenco dancer

◆ **LOOK AT THE BIG MAP.**
Can you see...
- five different wild animals?
- two tall mountain ranges?
- five different kinds of food?
- the Leaning Tower of Pisa?

26

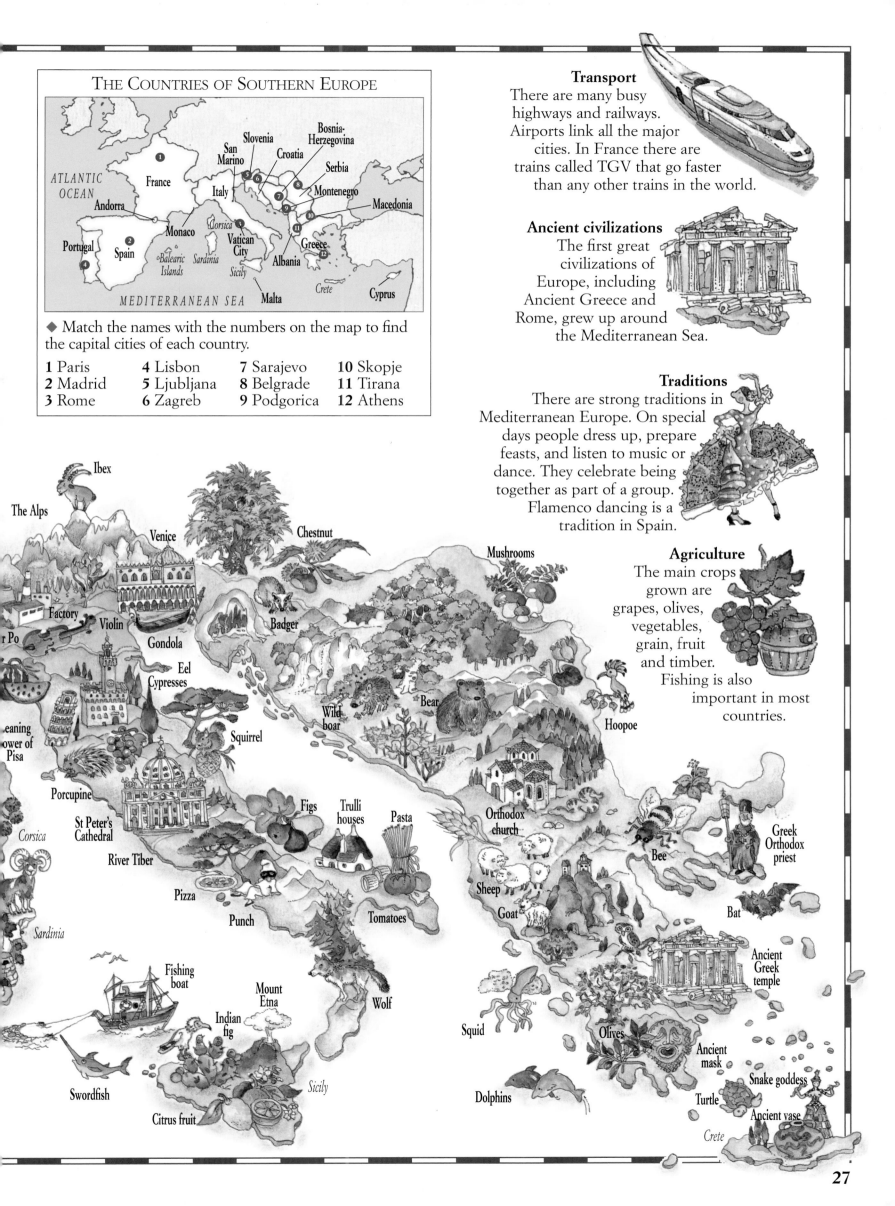

THE COUNTRIES OF SOUTHERN EUROPE

ATLANTIC OCEAN

France
Andorra
Portugal
Spain
Monaco
Corsica
Sardinia
Balearic Islands
San Marino
Slovenia
Croatia
Italy
Vatican City
Bosnia-Herzegovina
Serbia
Montenegro
Albania
Macedonia
Greece
Sicily
Crete
Malta
Cyprus

MEDITERRANEAN SEA

◆ Match the names with the numbers on the map to find the capital cities of each country.

1 Paris	**4** Lisbon	**7** Sarajevo	**10** Skopje
2 Madrid	**5** Ljubljana	**8** Belgrade	**11** Tirana
3 Rome	**6** Zagreb	**9** Podgorica	**12** Athens

Transport
There are many busy highways and railways. Airports link all the major cities. In France there are trains called TGV that go faster than any other trains in the world.

Ancient civilizations
The first great civilizations of Europe, including Ancient Greece and Rome, grew up around the Mediterranean Sea.

Traditions
There are strong traditions in Mediterranean Europe. On special days people dress up, prepare feasts, and listen to music or dance. They celebrate being together as part of a group. Flamenco dancing is a tradition in Spain.

Agriculture
The main crops grown are grapes, olives, vegetables, grain, fruit and timber. Fishing is also important in most countries.

Ibex
The Alps
Venice
Chestnut
Mushrooms
Factory
Violin
Gondola
Badger
River Po
Eel
Cypresses
Wild boar
Bear
Hoopoe
Leaning Tower of Pisa
Squirrel
Porcupine
St Peter's Cathedral
Corsica
Figs
Trulli houses
Pasta
Orthodox church
Bee
Greek Orthodox priest
River Tiber
Sheep
Goat
Bat
Pizza
Punch
Tomatoes
Sardinia
Ancient Greek temple
Fishing boat
Mount Etna
Wolf
Indian fig
Squid
Olives
Ancient mask
Snake goddess
Swordfish
Citrus fruit
Sicily
Dolphins
Turtle
Ancient vase
Crete

Eastern Europe

Russia is the biggest country in eastern Europe – in fact, only part of Russia is in Europe and the rest stretches east across Asia towards the Pacific Ocean. In the west, along the Baltic Sea, are the small states of Latvia, Lithuania and Estonia. Many people in this region work in factories in towns and cities. Farming is important in southern Russia, on the steppes (plains). Russian is the main language, although the people of the Baltic States have their own languages.

◆ **LOOK AT THE BIG MAP.**
Can you find…
• a traditional musical instrument called the balalaika?
• five agricultural products?
• five farm animals?
• three different churches?
• ten different wild animals?

Wildlife

Elks, bears, wolves and smaller animals, such as sable and martens, live in the great northern forests. Foxes, bustards and eagles live on the steppes. Small mammals, such as marmots, live in burrows to escape the keen eyes of predators on the open plains.

Moscow

Moscow is the capital of Russia. The famous Kremlin is a collection of palaces and cathedrals which were built in the fifteenth century. It is the traditional centre of the Russian government. Outside the Kremlin is Red Square, where parades are held to mark the Communist Revolution in 1917. The body of Lenin, the first Communist ruler, is preserved in a mausoleum here.

Industries

Russia has many of the raw materials needed to develop heavy industry and manufacturing: coal, gas and oil for power, and iron ore for making steel. Russian factories produce heavy machinery, such as farm equipment, railway engines and cars. Mining for minerals such as cobalt, lead and zinc is also important.

Russian ballet

Russian ballet dancers are among the best in the world. Dancers of the Bolshoi and Kirov companies perform ballets such as Swan Lake and The Sleeping Beauty. The music for many ballets was written by Tchaikovsky, a Russian composer.

The Cossacks

The Cossacks lived in southern Russia, around the Don and Volga rivers. They were famous for their skill as soldiers and horsemen. They were also famous for their energetic dances. They would squat down with arms folded and fling out their legs. Sometimes they danced with swords.

THE COUNTRIES OF EASTERN EUROPE

◆ Match the names with the numbers on the map to find the capital cities of each country.

1 Moscow	7 Chisinau
2 Tallinn	8 Bucharest
3 Riga	9 Sofia
4 Vilnius	10 Tbilisi
5 Minsk	11 Yerevan
6 Kiev	12 Baku

Caviar
Caviar – the salty eggs, or 'roe', of fish called sturgeon – is a great delicacy. It is a very expensive food. The finest caviar comes from the sturgeon of the Caspian Sea.

The summers in eastern Europe are mild but winters are cold and snowy. The far north of Russia is bitterly cold. The Ural Mountains mark the boundary between Europe and Asia. Half of Russia is covered in coniferous forests – the taiga. Major rivers such as the Don and the Volga flow south to the Black Sea. The steppes in the south of the region are good for growing wheat and other cereal crops.

Reindeer
Harp seal
Reindeer
Lemmings
Tern
Ship
Big bluebill
Arctic hare
Dwarf birch
Arctic fox
Ptarmigan
Scorpion fish
Elk
Northern hawk owl
Redshank
Ural Mountains
Northern Dvina River
Mink
Salmon
Chess board
Balalaika
Deer
Shelducks
Eagle
St Petersburg
Matrioshka dolls
Stave church
Wood grouse
Brown bears
Weasel
Ferry
Mines
Russian wolf hound
Tallinn
Sea
Silver birch trees
Marten
Industry
Riga
Icon
Oil
Gold
Flax
Beet
Dacia
Long-eared bat
Potatoes
Pike
Coal
Factory
Pigs
St Basil's Cathedral
Russian ballet
Samovar
Wheat
Cow
Vodka
Coal
Russian Orthodox priest
Shrew
Farmhouse
Hamster
Beaver
Geese
Wheat
Sunflower
Corn
Castor oil plant
Viper
Kiev
Cossacks
Monastery
Port of Odessa
River Volga
Volgograd
Religion
The Russian Orthodox Church is a branch of Christianity. It has been the main religion in Russia for over 1,000 years. Many Russian Christians have icons – small paintings of saints or of Mary and the baby Jesus – in their homes, which they use as a focus for their prayers.
River Don
Coal
Industry
Gas
Bucharest
Pelican
Rose
Porpoise
Castle
Shepherd
Sturgeon
Fishing
Tourism
Caspian Sea
Cruise boat
Black Sea
Tobacco
Tea
Fruit
Rugs
Sheep
Oil rigs
Perch
Cotton

29

Northern Africa

Most of northern Africa is covered by the Sahara Desert. The majority of people live near the coasts where it is not too hot or dry. To the north, most people speak the Arabic language, although French and English are common too. Islam is the main religion. Many people live in the country and work as farmers, although there are also some very large cities. Cairo, the capital city of Egypt, is the largest city in Africa.

The Sahara Desert
The Sahara is the largest desert in the world. It covers more than a quarter of the African continent. It is growing larger every year.

The Islamic religion
The majority of people in northern Africa are Muslims. They believe in Allah and follow the Islamic religion. There are loud calls to prayer five times each day. Believers kneel on prayer mats, facing towards Mecca in Saudi Arabia, and touch their heads on the ground as they pray. There are many beautiful mosques.

THE COUNTRIES OF NORTHERN AFRICA

◆ Match the names with the numbers on the map to find the capital cities of each country.

1 Rabat	9 Niamey
2 Algiers	10 Bamako
3 Tunis	11 Nouakchott
4 Tripoli	12 Djibouti
5 Cairo	13 Asmara
6 Khartoum	14 Mogadishu
7 Addis Ababa	15 Ouagadougou
8 Ndjamena	16 El Aaiún

Map labels: Canary Islands, Morocco, Tunisia, MEDITERRANEAN SEA, Western Sahara, Algeria, Libya, Egypt, Mauritania, Mali, Niger, Chad, Sudan, Cape Verde, Burkina Faso, RED SEA, Eritrea, Djibouti, Somalia, Ethiopia, ATLANTIC OCEAN

The first people
Africa is sometimes called the 'cradle of humanity' because traces of the first human beings have been found there. Many objects, like the stone cutter above, date to millions of years ago.

◆ **LOOK AT THE BIG MAP.**
Can you find…
- the Red Sea?
- the Ancient Egyptian sphinx?
- four desert animals?
- two different mosques?
- five different agricultural products?
- a Tuareg man on a camel?
- the Suez Canal?

Caravans in the desert
One-humped camels are native to northern Africa. They have been used for transport and travel since earliest times. Camels are so well suited to life in the desert that they are sometimes called 'ships of the desert'. Today, motor vehicles and aeroplanes are also used to cross the desert.

Desert animals
Many animals make their home in the desert. They have special features which help them to survive the heat during the day and the extreme cold at night.

Market day
On market day people bring farm products to sell in the local town or village. In many parts of Africa, women grow the crops and sell them.

Sponges

Indian fig

…an ruins

Olives

Natural gas

Oasis

Scorpion

Jackal

Fennec fox

Well

Falcon

Hedgehog

Acacia tree

Caravan

Cattle

Locust

Gerbil

Mummy

Cairo

Pyramids

Sphinx

Mosque

Suez Canal

Aswan Dam

Red Sea

Coral

Tropical fish

Ibis

Sheep and goats

Termite hill

Aardvark

Monitor lizard

River Nile

Nile fish

Crocodile

Waterfall

Shoe bill

Dragon tree

Papyrus

Python

Coffee

Ostrich

Sugar-cane

River Juba

Monkey

Ethiopian priest

Mastigure

Ass

Wild boar

Leopard

Bananas

Dhow

Incense tree

Southern Africa

Most people in southern Africa live in the country. They earn their living as farmers by growing crops and raising cattle. Many others live in cities. They work in shops, offices, factories and mines. They speak many different languages. Southern Africa has huge forests and savannas with many wild animals, including elephants, lions, giraffes, chimpanzees and gorillas.

Sugar-cane · Cattle egret · Buffalo · Masks · Cocoa · Leopard · Hornbill · Fisherman · Bananas · Elephant · Mangrove · Fish · Barracuda

Wildlife reserves

Many wild animals live in nature reserves where they are protected. People from all over the world visit Africa to see the animals.

The first humans

Africa is the birthplace of humans. The first people lived in Kenya and Tanzania millions of years ago. From here they spread all over the world. Rock paintings left by early peoples tell us something about their life.

Primal religions

Many African people believe in a world of spirits and gods. They have special ceremonies, with dance and song to worship the gods. Sometimes they wear masks during these ceremonies.

Madagascar

The huge island of Madagascar lies off the coast of southern Africa. It has been isolated from the continent for millions of years. It has unique plants and animals. The ring-tailed lemur, a distant relative of the monkey, lives only on Madagascar.

THE COUNTRIES OF SOUTHERN AFRICA

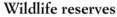

Gambia · Senegal · Togo · Benin · Central African Republic · Guinea-Bisseau · Ghana · Guinea · Nigeria · Sierra Leone · Equatorial Guinea · Cameroon · Uganda · Rwanda · Liberia · Ivory Coast · Sao Tomé & Príncipe · Gabon · Democratic Republic of the Congo · Kenya · Burundi · Congo · Tanzania · Seychelles · Angola · Malawi · ATLANTIC OCEAN · Zambia · Comoros · Madagascar · Namibia · Mozambique · Mauritius · Botswana · Zimbabwe · South Africa · Swaziland · INDIAN OCEAN · Lesotho

◆ There are thirty-three countries in southern Africa. The biggest is the Democratic Republic of the Congo. South Africa is the richest. Madagascar is a large island that was once part of Africa. The red dots with numbers in them on the map above show some of the largest cities in this part of the world. Find the number on the map to see where they are.

1 Yamoussoukro
2 Kinshasa
3 Luanda
4 Cape Town
5 Johannesburg
6 Maputo
7 Lusaka
8 Dodoma
9 Nairobi
10 Antananarivo

Southern Africa, also called sub-Saharan Africa, lies below the Sahara Desert, and between the Indian and Atlantic oceans. There is tropical rainforest near the Equator. Further south there are grasslands (called savanna) and deserts. The climate is hot or warm with enough rain, except in the Namib and Kalahari deserts which are very dry. The largest rivers are the Congo, the Zambezi and the Niger.

◆ **LOOK AT THE BIG MAP.**
Can you find…
• a traditional African village?
• ten different wild animals?
• two large rivers?
• three different masks?
• five different trees?
• Victoria Falls?
• Mount Kilimanjaro?

Mineral wealth
Many countries have rich deposits of minerals, such as copper, gold, tin and diamonds.

Millet

Pelican

Crocodile

Musical instruments

Euphorbia

Lion

Flamingo

Snake

Okapi

Gorilla

Agave

Coffee

Mount Kilimanjaro

Wildebeest

Chimpanzee

Vulture

Rainforest

Palm

Marabou

Acacia tree

Gazelle

Turtle

Hippopotamus

Zebra

Cotton

Oxpecker

River Congo

Anteater

Giraffe

Sting ray

Rhinoceros

Victoria Falls

Cobra

Bottle tree

Chameleon

Traveller's tree

Oryx

Leopard

Namib Desert

Crane

Baobab

Cheetah

River Zambezi

Quiver tree

African hunting dog

Vanilla

Traditional village

Tobacco

Seals

Cactus

Rock paintings

Lemur

Penguin

Diamond

Humpback whale

Grapes

Outrigger canoe

Ostriches

Fish

Gold

Matze

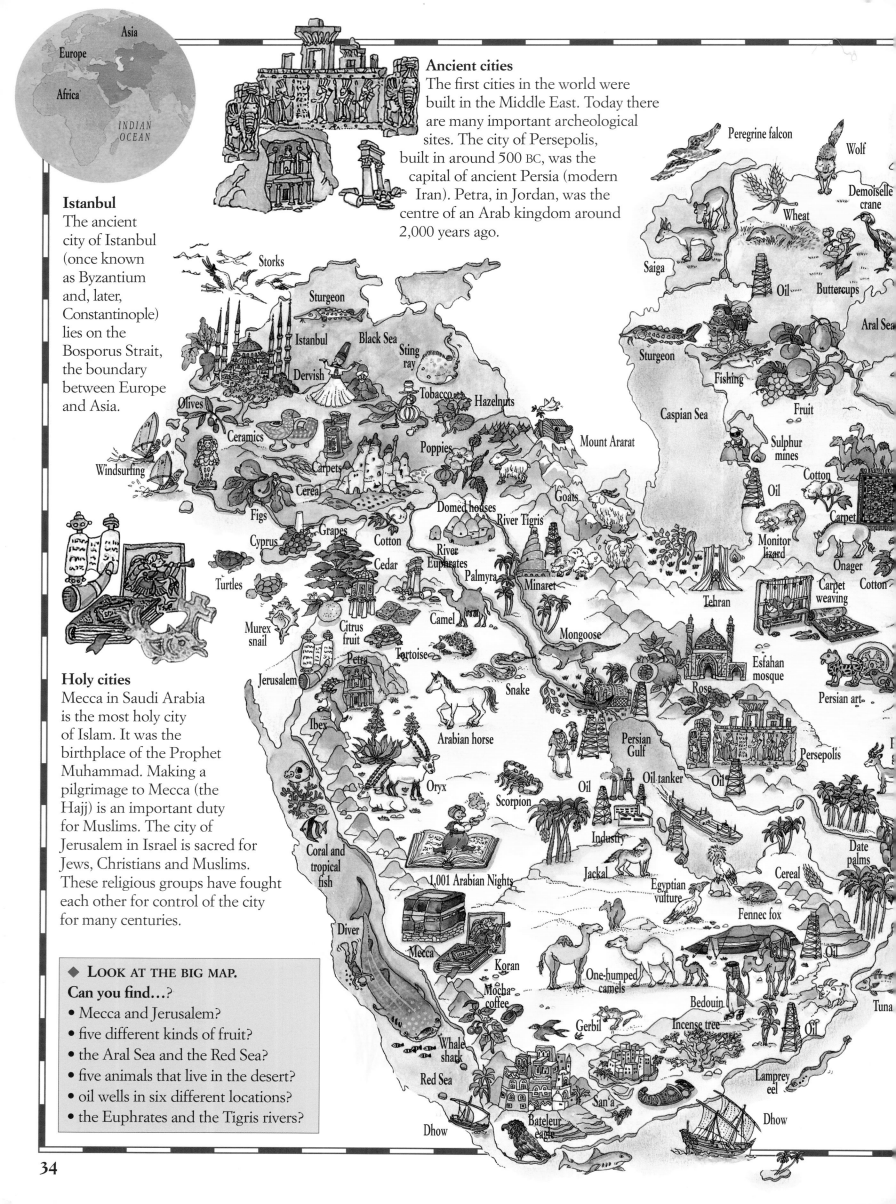

Ancient cities

The first cities in the world were built in the Middle East. Today there are many important archeological sites. The city of Persepolis, built in around 500 BC, was the capital of ancient Persia (modern Iran). Petra, in Jordan, was the centre of an Arab kingdom around 2,000 years ago.

Istanbul

The ancient city of Istanbul (once known as Byzantium and, later, Constantinople) lies on the Bosporus Strait, the boundary between Europe and Asia.

Holy cities

Mecca in Saudi Arabia is the most holy city of Islam. It was the birthplace of the Prophet Muhammad. Making a pilgrimage to Mecca (the Hajj) is an important duty for Muslims. The city of Jerusalem in Israel is sacred for Jews, Christians and Muslims. These religious groups have fought each other for control of the city for many centuries.

◆ LOOK AT THE BIG MAP.
Can you find…?
• Mecca and Jerusalem?
• five different kinds of fruit?
• the Aral Sea and the Red Sea?
• five animals that live in the desert?
• oil wells in six different locations?
• the Euphrates and the Tigris rivers?

Map labels:
Asia, Europe, Africa, INDIAN OCEAN
Peregrine falcon, Wolf, Demoiselle crane, Wheat, Saiga, Oil, Buttercups, Aral Sea, Sturgeon, Fishing, Fruit, Caspian Sea, Sulphur mines, Cotton, Oil, Carpet, Monitor lizard, Onager, Cotton, Carpet weaving, Tehran, Esfahan mosque, Rose, Persian art, Persepolis
Storks, Sturgeon, Istanbul, Black Sea, Sting ray, Dervish, Tobacco, Hazelnuts, Olives, Ceramics, Poppies, Mount Ararat, Carpets, Cereal, Domed houses, River Tigris, Goats, Windsurfing, Figs, Grapes, Cotton, River Euphrates, Palmyra, Minaret, Mongoose
Cyprus, Cedar, Camel, Snake, Turtles, Citrus fruit, Tortoise, Arabian horse, Murex snail, Petra, Jerusalem, Ibex, Oryx, Scorpion, Oil, Persian Gulf, Oil tanker, Oil
Coral and tropical fish, 1,001 Arabian Nights, Industry, Jackal, Egyptian vulture, Date palms, Cereal, Fennec fox, Oil
Diver, Mecca, Koran, Mocha coffee, One-humped camels, Bedouin, Incense tree, Gerbil, Tuna, Whale shark, Red Sea, San'a, Lamprey eel, Dhow, Bateleur eagle, Dhow

34

The Middle East and Central Asia

Much of the Middle East is very hot and dry, so most people live where they can find water. Many people work as farmers. Others work in the oil industry, especially in Saudi Arabia and the countries around the Persian Gulf. Most of the Middle Eastern peoples are Arabs. Their religion is Islam. The modern country of Israel was founded in 1948. It is a Jewish nation. The peoples of central Asia are mainly Muslims. Most live as farmers, although industry is growing too.

Labels on map illustration: Bobacs, Cereals, Cereals, Sand-grouse, Golden hamster, Sunflower, Mining, Gold, Mines, Krangs, Lake Balkhash, Shepherd, Space base, Ground squirrel, Goats, Sheep, Yak, Desert dormouse, Samarkand, Industry, Nomads' tents, Bearded vulture, Lapis lazuli, Afghan hound, Antelope, Nomads' tents, Cotton, Pallas cat, Carpet

Oil

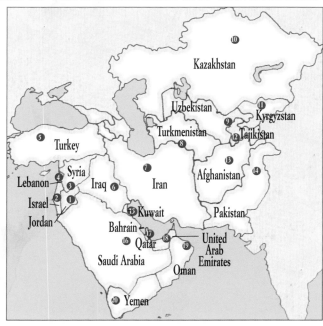

Around the Persian Gulf oil collects naturally in underground pools. Eight million barrels of oil a day are produced in Saudi Arabia, the region's biggest producer. It is transported by pipeline or in huge oil tankers to countries around the world. Oil has brought great wealth to some of the Middle Eastern states.

Hot, dry, sandy deserts cover large areas of the Middle East. When rain does fall, it often comes in heavy downpours which cause sudden floods. Summers are very hot, but in the central regions winters can be very cold. Along the Mediterranean coasts and in the valleys of the great Tigris and Euphrates rivers there is fertile land that is good for farming. The countries of central Asia have many deserts and high, rugged mountains.

Growing cotton

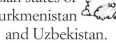

Cotton production is an important industry in the central Asian states of Tajikistan, Turkmenistan and Uzbekistan.

Bazaars

Markets in Middle Eastern towns are called bazaars. Twisting narrow streets are crowded with traders selling their wares. Bazaars are often covered by canopies or a roof, to protect people from the hot sun.

The Countries of the Middle East and Central Asia

◆ Match the names with the numbers on the map to find the capital cities of each country.

1 Amman
2 Jerusalem
3 Damascus
4 Beirut
5 Ankara
6 Baghdad
7 Tehran
8 Ashkhabad
9 Tashkent
10 Astana
11 Bishkek
12 Dushanbe
13 Kabul
14 Islamabad
15 Kuwait City
16 Riyadh
17 Doha
18 Abu Dhabi
19 Muscat
20 San'a

Map labels: Kazakhstan, Uzbekistan, Kyrgyzstan, Turkey, Turkmenistan, Tajikistan, Syria, Afghanistan, Lebanon, Iraq, Iran, Israel, Jordan, Kuwait, Pakistan, Bahrain, Qatar, United Arab Emirates, Saudi Arabia, Oman, Yemen

Eastern Asia

More than one-fifth of the world's entire population lives in China. Although the crowded cities are growing, most people still live in villages. China is a Communist country and until recently farms and industries were run by the government. The cold lands of Siberia, which are part of Russia, lie to the north of China. Coal mining and drilling for oil and gas are important industries here. In Japan, most people work in factories, shops and offices. Many of the factories produce high-tech electronic equipment.

◆ **LOOK AT THE BIG MAP.**
Can you find…
• a two-humped camel?
• the Great Wall of China?
• a Tibetan prayer wheel?
• Hong Kong?
• the Yellow River?

Tibet
Tibet is famous for the Buddhist monks who play an important part in the traditional way of life. The religious leader, the Dalai Lama, was also the political leader. China took over Tibet in 1951. In 1959 China forced the Dalai Lama to live in exile (outside the country).

THE COUNTRIES OF EASTERN ASIA
◆ Find the capital cities of each country.

1 Ulan Bator	4 Seoul
2 Beijing	5 Tokyo
3 Pyongyang	6 Taipei

The climate of eastern Asia ranges from bitterly cold in the far north to hot and wet in the far south. Much of Siberia is cold, treeless tundra. Further south, in China, there are large deserts – the Gobi and the Takla Makan. In the south-west are the Himalayan mountains and the world's highest mountain, Everest. The Yangtze River and the Yellow River flow across eastern China. The islands of Japan are mountainous and covered in dense forests. Earthquakes are a danger in this area.

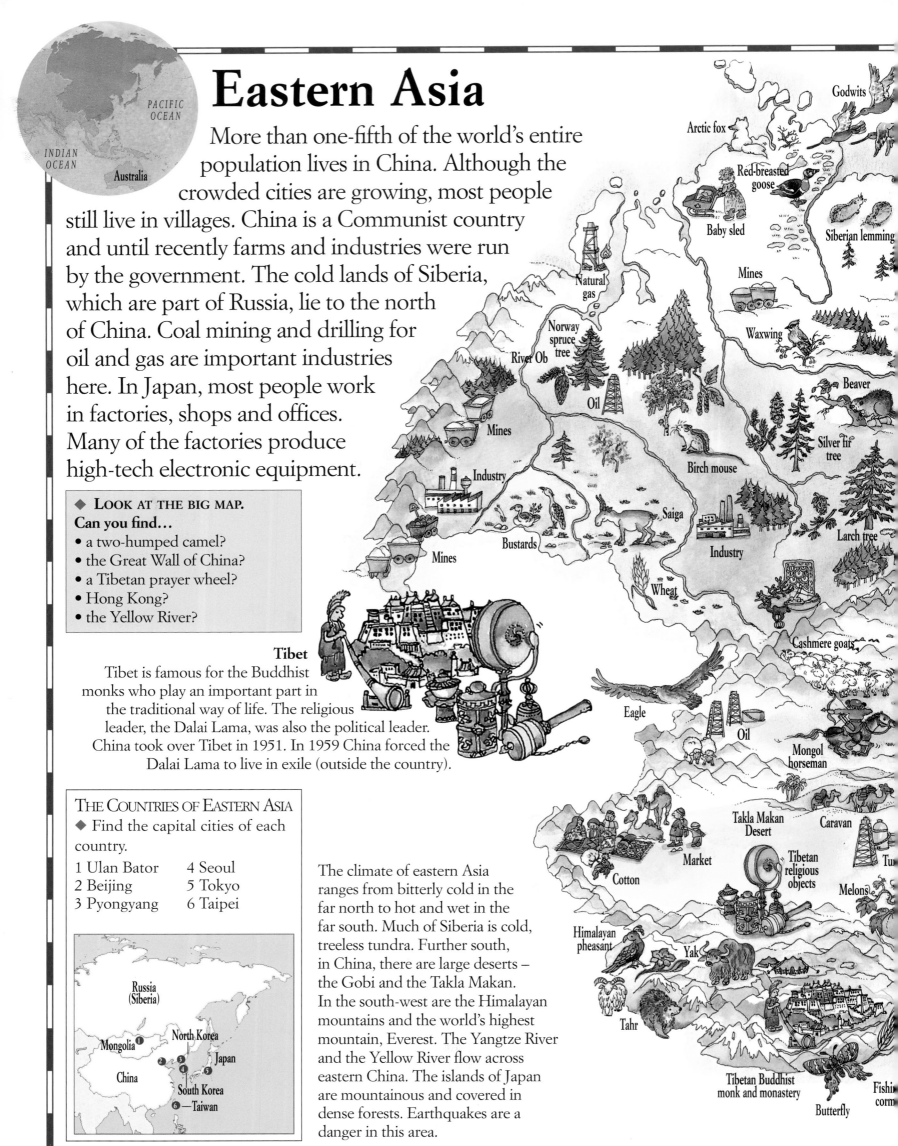

Polar bear
Supply ship
Chukchi artefacts
Walrus
Otter
Seal
Snowy owl
Polar bear
River Lena
Chukchi
Ermine
Gold
Wolves
Reindeer
Glutton
Seals
Brown bear
Volcanoes
Sea of Okhotsk
nonds
Black grouse
Grey whale
Goral
Racoon dog
Japanese cranes
Timber
Sable
Bonsai
Lake Baikal
Baikal seal
Pigs
ber
Geese
Siberian tigers
Trans-Siberian Railway
Kites
Wild horses
Timber
Squirrel
Ginkgo tree
Macaques
Coal
Spider crab
Two-humped camel
Industry
Jade artefacts
Fish
Kabuki theatre
Porcelain
Ginseng
Pagoda
Beijing
Shinto shrine
Mount Fuji
Great Wall of China
Sampan boat
Pearl fishing
Chinese theatre
Chow chow
Ship building
Junk
Giant salamander
Terracotta Army
Wheat
Alligator
Silk worms
Tea
Bamboo
Golden pheasant
Mandarin duck
Yellow River
River dolphin
Port of Shanghai
Takin
usk
eer
Table tennis
Chop sticks
High-tech industries
Giant panda
Tree shrew
Buffalo
Hong Kong
Mines
Paddy fields
Fisherman
Stone forest
Rice

Martial arts

Many people enjoy watching the enormous sumo wrestlers of Japan. Other martial arts such as judo, aikido and karate have become popular sports in many parts of the world. People learn how to defend themselves using only their bodies, instead of using weapons.

Shinto

Shinto is the traditional religion of Japan. Followers of Shinto believe that the Japanese emperors are descended from the sun goddess, Amaterasu Omikami. One of the Shinto festivals is called Shichi-go-san (seven-five-three). At this festival, children aged seven, five and three thank the gods for protecting them and pray for healthy lives in the future.

Terracotta Army

China's 'terracotta army' is a collection of over 6,000 life-size terracotta models of soldiers, horses and chariots. They were found in the tomb of the first emperor of all China, Shih huang-ti, who came to power in 221 BC.

Hong Kong

Hong Kong was ruled by Britain for almost 100 years. The small territory became an important centre for business and international trade. In 1997, control of Hong Kong was handed back to China.

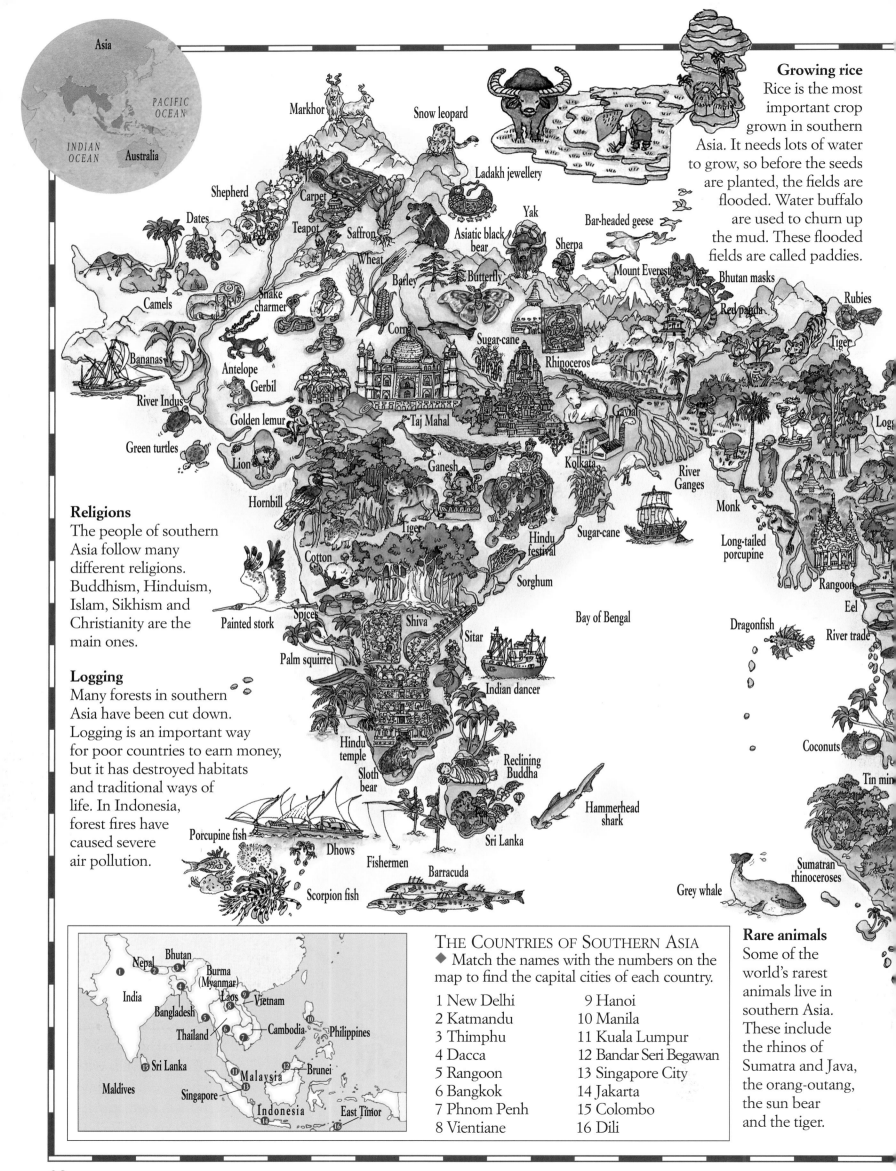

Growing rice
Rice is the most important crop grown in southern Asia. It needs lots of water to grow, so before the seeds are planted, the fields are flooded. Water buffalo are used to churn up the mud. These flooded fields are called paddies.

Religions
The people of southern Asia follow many different religions. Buddhism, Hinduism, Islam, Sikhism and Christianity are the main ones.

Logging
Many forests in southern Asia have been cut down. Logging is an important way for poor countries to earn money, but it has destroyed habitats and traditional ways of life. In Indonesia, forest fires have caused severe air pollution.

Rare animals
Some of the world's rarest animals live in southern Asia. These include the rhinos of Sumatra and Java, the orang-outang, the sun bear and the tiger.

THE COUNTRIES OF SOUTHERN ASIA
◆ Match the names with the numbers on the map to find the capital cities of each country.

1 New Delhi
2 Katmandu
3 Thimphu
4 Dacca
5 Rangoon
6 Bangkok
7 Phnom Penh
8 Vientiane
9 Hanoi
10 Manila
11 Kuala Lumpur
12 Bandar Seri Begawan
13 Singapore City
14 Jakarta
15 Colombo
16 Dili

Labels on map: Asia, PACIFIC OCEAN, INDIAN OCEAN, Australia, Markhor, Snow leopard, Ladakh jewellery, Shepherd, Carpet, Teapot, Saffron, Dates, Wheat, Barley, Butterfly, Yak, Asiatic black bear, Sherpa, Bar-headed geese, Mount Everest, Bhutan masks, Rubies, Red panda, Tiger, Snake charmer, Camels, Corn, Sugar-cane, Rhinoceros, Antelope, Gerbil, Taj Mahal, Gavial, River Ganges, Bananas, Golden lemur, Ganesh, Kolkata, Monk, River Indus, Green turtles, Lion, Sugar-cane, Long-tailed porcupine, Rangoon, Eel, Hornbill, Tiger, Hindu festival, Dragonfish, River trade, Cotton, Sorghum, Bay of Bengal, Painted stork, Spice, Shiva, Sitar, Palm squirrel, Indian dancer, Coconuts, Tin mine, Hindu temple, Sloth bear, Reclining Buddha, Porcupine fish, Dhows, Fishermen, Barracuda, Sri Lanka, Hammerhead shark, Sumatran rhinoceroses, Scorpion fish, Grey whale

Inset map labels: Nepal, Bhutan, Burma (Myanmar), India, Laos, Vietnam, Bangladesh, Thailand, Cambodia, Philippines, Sri Lanka, Malaysia, Brunei, Maldives, Singapore, Indonesia, East Timor

Southern Asia

Fishing
People in southern Asia eat more fish than meat. In some areas people go out in outrigger canoes to catch fish for their families. In others, large fishing boats are used to catch thousands of fish at a time. A lot of the fish is sold to other countries.

Southern Asia's cities are growing. People have moved to cities such as Kolkata, Mumbai, Jakarta and Manila in search of work. There are more and more factories making cars, electronic equipment and textiles. Despite this, there are still many more farmers than factory workers in southern Asia. The peoples of this region are descended from people who moved from the north of the continent many centuries ago. Many different languages are spoken.

Much of southern Asia is hilly or mountainous and covered with dense jungle. There are volcanoes on many of the islands. There is good farmland on the flat land near river deltas, such as the Ganges in India and Bangladesh. The climate is hot and humid all year round and during the monsoon seasons there is very heavy rain.

Pagoda
Poppies
River boat
Paddy fields
Terrace farming
Bat
Monkey-eating eagle
Outrigger canoe
Volcanic islands
Nautilus
Tree shrew
Flying squirrel
Moonrat
mese ing fish
Archerfish
Kapok tree
Oil
Oyster farming
Mandarin fish
Breadfruit tree
Tree house
Butterfly fish
Stilt village
Crocodile
Angel fish
Sharks
Clown fish
Toradja house
Rubber trees
Gibbon
Mask
Banded linsang
Singapore
Bearded pig
Proboscis monkey
Orang-outang
Butterfly
Bat
Cloves
Pig
Rat
Crab-eating monkey
Rafflesia
Nutmeg
Bird of Paradise
Otter civet
Manioca
Moon fish
Sail fish
Shadow puppet
Mudskipper
Prao
Tapir
Komodo dragon
oo
Volcanoes
Javan rhinoceros
Buddha
Batik
Dancer
Red jungle fowl
Pepper

◆ **LOOK AT THE BIG MAP.**
Can you find…
- the River Ganges?
- seven different kinds of fish?
- a Komodo dragon?
- Singapore?
- a sitar?
- the Taj Mahal?

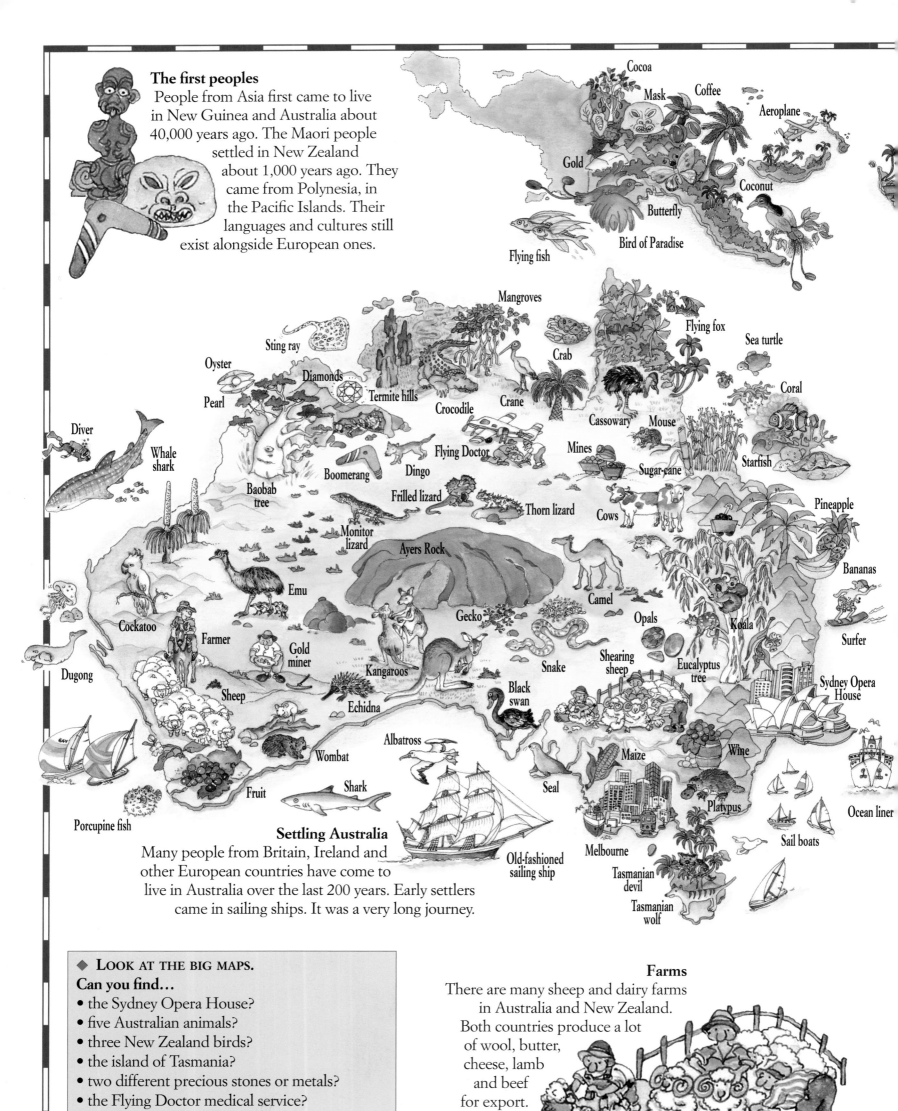

The first peoples

People from Asia first came to live in New Guinea and Australia about 40,000 years ago. The Maori people settled in New Zealand about 1,000 years ago. They came from Polynesia, in the Pacific Islands. Their languages and cultures still exist alongside European ones.

Cocoa
Mask
Coffee
Aeroplane
Gold
Coconut
Butterfly
Bird of Paradise
Flying fish

Mangroves
Flying fox
Sea turtle
Sting ray
Crab
Oyster
Coral
Diamonds
Termite hills
Crane
Pearl
Crocodile
Cassowary
Mouse
Diver
Flying Doctor
Mines
Starfish
Whale shark
Sugar-cane
Boomerang
Dingo
Baobab tree
Frilled lizard
Thorn lizard
Cows
Pineapple
Monitor lizard
Ayers Rock
Camel
Bananas
Emu
Cockatoo
Gecko
Opals
Koala
Farmer
Camel
Surfer
Gold miner
Snake
Shearing sheep
Eucalyptus tree
Dugong
Kangaroos
Sydney Opera House
Sheep
Black swan
Echidna
Wombat
Albatross
Maize
Wine
Fruit
Shark
Seal
Platypus
Ocean liner
Porcupine fish
Melbourne
Sail boats
Old-fashioned sailing ship
Tasmanian devil
Tasmanian wolf

Settling Australia

Many people from Britain, Ireland and other European countries have come to live in Australia over the last 200 years. Early settlers came in sailing ships. It was a very long journey.

◆ LOOK AT THE BIG MAPS.
Can you find…
• the Sydney Opera House?
• five Australian animals?
• three New Zealand birds?
• the island of Tasmania?
• two different precious stones or metals?
• the Flying Doctor medical service?
• two kangaroos boxing?

Farms

There are many sheep and dairy farms in Australia and New Zealand. Both countries produce a lot of wool, butter, cheese, lamb and beef for export.

Australasia

Most people in Australia and New Zealand live in towns and cities. There are also many farms, and agriculture is important for both countries. The majority of people speak English. There are many immigrants from all over the world. Papua New Guinea is the eastern half of the island of New Guinea. Many Papuans live in traditional ways in country villages, just as their ancestors have done for thousands of years.

Great Barrier Reef

The Great Barrier Reef is made of brightly coloured coral. It is the largest reef in the world and stretches 2,120 km down the east coast of Australia. The warm tropical waters near the reef are teeming with fish and other animals.

Special animals

There are some unique animals in Australia and New Zealand. Some, like kangaroos, koalas and opossums, have pouches on their tummies for carrying their babies. They are called marsupials. Others, like kiwis and emus, are birds that cannot fly.

Australasia is made up of the islands of Australia, New Zealand and Papua New Guinea. Northern Australia and Papua have hot tropical climates. Central Australia has many large deserts. Southern Australia and New Zealand have cooler, temperate weather.

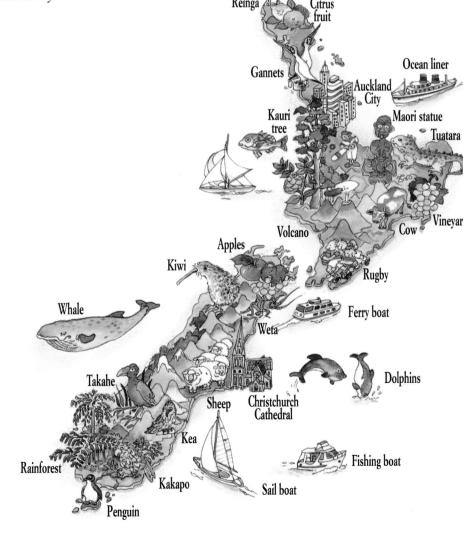

Cape Reinga · Citrus fruit · Gannets · Ocean liner · Auckland City · Kauri tree · Maori statue · Tuatara · Volcano · Apples · Cow · Vineyards · Kiwi · Rugby · Whale · Ferry boat · Weta · Dolphins · Takahe · Sheep · Christchurch Cathedral · Fishing boat · Kea · Rainforest · Kakapo · Sail boat · Penguin

THE COUNTRIES OF AUSTRALASIA

◆ Find the capital cities of each country.

1 Canberra   2 Wellington   3 Port Moresby

Palau · Micronesia · Papua New Guinea · Marshall Islands · Kiribati · Nauru · Solomon Islands · Tuvalu · Vanuatu · Samoan Islands · Fiji · Tonga · PACIFIC OCEAN · INDIAN OCEAN · Australia · SOUTHERN OCEAN · Tasmania · North Island · New Zealand · South Island

Tasmania is a part of Australia. New Zealand is divided into North Island and South Island.

Index

43

 **Cyprus** Nicosia

 **Bulgaria** Sofia

 **Romania** Bucharest

 **Estonia** Tallinn

 **Latvia** Riga

 **Lithuania** Vilnius

 **Belarus** Minsk

 **Ukraine** Kiev

 **Moldova** Chisinau

 **Georgia** Tbilisi

 **Armenia** Yerevan

 **Azerbaijan** Baku

 **Russia** Moscow

 **Turkey** Ankara

 **Israel** Jerusalem

 **Lebanon** Beirut

 **Jordan** Amman

 **Syria** Damascus

 **Saudi Arabia** Riyadh

 **Yemen** San'a

 **Oman** Muscat

 **United Arab Emirates** Abu Dhabi

 **Bahrain** Manama

 **Qatar** Doha

 **Kuwait** Kuwait City

 **Iraq** Baghdad

 **Iran** Tehran

 **Turkmenistan** Ashkhabad

 **Afghanistan** Kabul

 **Uzbekistan** Tashkent

 **Kazakhstan** Astana

 **Tajikistan** Dushanbe

 **Kyrgyzstan** Bishkek

 **Pakistan** Islamabad

 **India** New Delhi

 Nepal Katmandu

 **Bhutan** Thimphu

 **Bangladesh** Dhaka

 **Sri Lanka** Colombo

 **The Maldives** Malé

 **China** Beijing

 **Mongolia** Ulan Bator

 **Japan** Tokyo

 **North Korea** Pyongyang

 **South Korea** Seoul

 **Taiwan** Taipei

 **Burma (Myanmar)** Rangoon

 **Thailand** Bangkok

 **Laos** Vientiane

 **Vietnam** Hanoi

 **Cambodia** Phnom Penh

 **Malaysia** Kuala Lumpur

 **Singapore** Singapore City

 **Indonesia** Jakarta

 **Brunei** Bandar Seri Begawan

 **The Philippines** Manila

 **Morocco** Rabat

 **Algeria** Algiers

 **Tunisia** Tunis

 **Libya** Tripoli

 **Egypt** Cairo

 **Western Sahara** El Aaiún

 **Mauritania** Nouakchott